Counting Caterpillars

and Other Math Poems

by Betsy Franco

SCHOLASTIC
PROFESSIONAL **B**OOKS

New York • Toronto • London • Auckland • Sydney • Mexico City • New Delhi • Hong Kong

Dedication

For my dad, who kept me laughing

Edited by Sarah Glasscock

Cover design by Jaime Lucero

Cover art by Jane Conte Morgan

Interior Design by Ellen Matlach Hassell
for Boultinghouse & Boultinghouse, Inc.

Interior art by Maxie Chambliss

ISBN: 0-590-64210-3

Contents

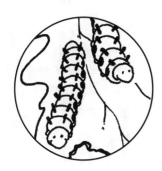

Introduction

Rhyming poetry is a perfect platter for serving math to young children.
Poems tickle children and bring out the fun and giggles in mathematics.
Poetry can provide an everyday, fanciful, or silly context for math ideas and
transform problem solving into a puzzle or game. Through their rhythm and
rhyming patterns, poems even mimic the patterns in math.

There's no doubt that poetry adds that extra beat to the comprehension of
mathematical skills that brings out the best in children. Poems demonstrate
that mathematics is a beautiful, joyful, rhythmic source of fun!

How Is the Book Organized?

Three suggestions for each poem help you make the most of the poetry, from
a mathematical as well as a language arts point of view. The first suggestion is
designed to determine children's prior knowledge. More important, it allows
children to interact with each poem and make it their own. They may predict
rhymes, make word substitutions, recite predictable portions of the poem,
find number words, and much more.

Suggestions for hands-on math activities come next. Activities can be
completed as a whole class, in small groups, or in stations around the room.
It's up to you. Here, children may use a pocket chart to make patterns of col-
orful birds sitting on a telephone wire. They may nibble pretzel numerals.
They may grab "ants" from a paper bag and figure out if they have an odd or
even number of insects. They may make rows of veggies from vegetable prints
to explore pre-multiplication—and they may even try blowing cubic bubbles
from a square-shaped dipper!

The final suggestion has several applications that include home activities
to involve the family, literature links to math-related picture books, and powerful math extensions. You'll find that poetry is a lovely link for family members of all ages. Send home a copy of the poem with each home activity. It's a
subtle and effective way of showing parents the fun and joy in mathematics
and letting them share in their children's learning experiences.

How to Use the Collection

There are a multitude of ways to present the poetry. Children can keep math
poetry books with a copy of each poem. You can create pocket chart strips of
appropriate poems and use them in connection with your weekly poetry pro-
gram. Poems can be displayed on the overhead projector; they can be written
on chart paper, or made into tagboard posters with illustrations.

The table of contents shows you where each poem fits into your math
curriculum or into the themes you may teach throughout the year. Once you
get going, your children will look forward to the poetry link with each new
math concept they learn!

Stuffed Animal Lunch

We set our stuffed animals
up in a row—
a chimp and a lion,
a bear and a crow.
Each one got a hat
and a special balloon,
They each got a plate
and a cup and a spoon.
The bear ate too much,
and the chimp spilled the punch,
But they had a great time
at the animal lunch.

Counting Caterpillars and Other Math Poems Scholastic Professional Books

"Stuffed Animal Lunch"

One-to-One Correspondence

Playing with the Poem

Children love to talk about their favorite stuffed animals, so why not start the discussion there? Then prepare them for the most predictable part of the poem—the rhymes. By brainstorming words that rhyme with *row*, *spoon*, and *lunch*, children will feel like the rhyming words are old friends when the poem is read.

After reading the poem, ask children to name the items that each animal has. Emphasize the notion of *one for each* and discuss the fact that there are the same number of hats, balloons, cups, plates, and spoons (four) as there are animals.

If you re-create the poem on a pocket chart, combine the first two lines and last two lines. You may also choose to write the poem on chart paper. Encourage children to make word substitutions. For instance, cover the words *chimp* and *bear* with blank word cards and then write in other animal names that children suggest. Substitutions can also be done using chart paper and sticky notes.

Handfuls of Bears

Set out two colors of Teddy Bear counters or other animal counters and have each child grab a handful of each color counter. Challenge them to figure out if they have the same number of each color, *without counting*.

Younger children may enjoy a "stuffed animal lunch" with punch and a snack. They can bring in stuffed animals and make hats for the animals. Set out paper plates and cups and plastic spoons. Before children set the table, emphasize the notion of *one for each*. Circulate among them, and ask if there are the same number of animals as hats, and so on.

Making Matches at Home

With the help of someone at home, children should find two sets of items to match and compare (without counting). Send home a list of possible questions such as the following for parents or other family members to ask: *Are there the same number of spoons and forks in the silverware drawer? Are there the same number of pencils and pens in the desk drawer? Does Mom's purse have the same number of pennies and dimes in it?*

The Lost Blue Parakeet

There once was a birdie named Phoebe
who lived with my great Uncle Stevie.
She flew out the door,
and we saw her no more,
till we heard her outside chirping "Feed me."

She joined in the wild bird band
till I stuck out some food on my hand.
They sat red, red, blue,
Then our parakeet flew,
and another blue bird had to land.

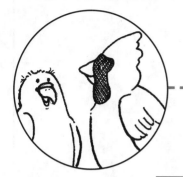

"The Lost Blue Parakeet"

Patterns

◨ Limerick Time

Write the first verse of the poem on chart paper or in a pocket chart. Introduce the word *limerick* to children and let it roll off their tongues. Explain that limericks are funny rhymes that often start by presenting someone to the reader. Ask children who is presented in the first line of this limerick. Then read and look over the first verse together. Ask children: *How many lines does the limerick have? Which lines rhyme?* Clap the beat with children. Talk about how many beats each line has. [3, 3, 2, 2, 3]

◨ Bird Patterns

Use the patterns on page 58 to cut out and color ten tagboard birds for a pocket chart. Remember that the smaller bird is Phoebe, the lost blue parakeet. After reading the second verse, let children line up the birds, including Phoebe, according to the pattern described in the poem (red, red, blue). One blue bird can be waiting on a higher row of the pocket chart. When Phoebe flies away to join her owner, this blue bird can come to take Phoebe's place in the pattern. Reinforce the AAB pattern of the birds by using claps and snaps or bird sounds such as *peep, peep, caw*.

◨ Plenty of Patterns

Of course, the birds may not always want to sit in the same pattern. Children can create other patterns (ABAB, ABC, BBA) using two or three colors of a particular manipulative such as color tiles or linking cubes. Once they have a pattern they like, encourage children to draw their patterns on paper. It will be more fun if they draw the pattern as birds sitting on a telephone wire.

My Good Old Backpack

My backpack has a rip in it,
But I don't really care.
It hops with me, it jumps with me,
It goes 'most everywhere.

Sometimes it's filled with school stuff,
or balls or special junk.
Sometimes my lunch bag opens up
and then it's full of gunk.

I tie on charms and key chains
so it jingles and it chimes.
Without my good old backpack,
I'd have an awful time.

Counting Caterpillars and Other Math Poems Scholastic Professional Books

Sorting

Getting Personal

Since backpacks adorn most schoolchildren's backs, children know them intimately. Make pocket chart strips for the first two verses of the poem so children can interact with the poem by substituting words from their own experiences. Then write the lines below on chart paper. Give children sticky notes and ask them to supply words for the blanks:

It _____ with me, it _____ with me,
Sometimes it's filled with _____
or _____ or special junk.

Sorting Backpacks

Hold a class sorting spree. Children can sort their backpacks by main color or number of colors, number of zippers, number of pockets, whether the backpack is decorated or not decorated, or by weight (for instance, less than three pounds or more than three pounds). After each sorting, have children count how many backpacks are in each group. Discuss which pile has the most and which has the least.

Line 'em Up

To go one intriguing step farther, make concrete graphs using the backpacks. Line them up instead of sorting them into piles. Better yet, create a permanent record by making a class wall graph. Each child can draw a picture of his or her backpack and glue it onto the graph. (A graphing pocket chart also works well.) The counting and comparing become more visual and easier to understand on a graph. Children can quickly figure out how many more backpacks are in one group than in another. You may also want to use the graph paper on page 59.

Snake Time

The snakes lined up
on measuring day,
I measured each one
before they could play.
They got in a row
in an orderly way,
Then shortest to longest
they slithered away.

Counting Caterpillars and Other Math Poems Scholastic Professional Books

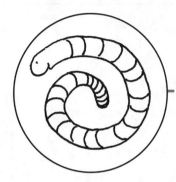

Comparing and Ordering

Snake Time Rhymes

Every one of the rhyming words in "Snake Time" has the *ay* sound. Pass out a copy of the poem to each child. As you read the poem aloud, have children find all the rhyming words and allow them to discover the pattern themselves. Make a list of the rhyming words that they find. Add other *ay* words that children suggest to the list. There are so many–*pay, say, may, tray, stay, okay, today*–and the list goes on!

Lining Up Snakes

Discuss the whimsical pictures that illustrates the poem. Ask children which snake is the longest, the next longest, and the shortest. If appropriate, they can measure their snakes using connecting cubes, rulers, or Inchworms. Coiled snakes can be measured with string or yarn. Then provide play dough so they can mold their own snake families. Naming the snakes can make this activity even more personal. Have children compare the lengths of their snakes and line them up in order. Again, they may use a variety of measuring tools to measure their snakes. Just warn children not to let the snakes eat the Inchworms!

Family Measuring Day

Homes are ideal places for comparing, ordering, and even measuring objects. Suggest one of the following at-home activities:

- Have children order the members of their family by height and draw a picture. Family members' heights can be measured and labeled in inches.

- Shoes and socks from different family members can also be ordered by length. Children can trace the shoes, bring their pictures to school, and compare lengths.

- For fun, ask children to compare and order the lengths of the first names in their families. That should stir up the order a bit!

Nibbling Pretzel Numbers

Nibble a 1,
Nibble a 2,
Nibble a 3, a 4, a 5.
Crunch at a pretzel here and there,
and watch how the numbers come alive.

Nibble a 6,
Nibble a 7,
Nibble an 8, a 9, a 10.
Then if you're hungry when you're done,
start with the 1 and do it again.

Counting Caterpillars and Other Math Poems Scholastic Professional Books

Writing Numerals

Predictable Pretzel Poem

Here's a tasty twist on writing numerals. Nibble a few numerals using twisted and stick pretzels and show them to children. Then display the poem where everyone can see it, on chart paper or in a pocket chart. As you read, hold up the pretzel numerals and encourage children to join in on the predictable lines of the poem that start with "Nibble a. . . ."

Nibbling Numerals

Have both twisted and stick pretzels available for nibbling numerals. Using the two kinds of pretzels together makes the job a lot easier, although it can be done with just one kind or the other. Warn children that a tiny bite on the pretzel here and there works better than a big crunch. A piece of construction paper can serve as a mat for each child so that everyone knows where her or his work space begins and ends. Talk about which numerals were harder or easier to create and why.

After all the creations have been properly admired, let children devour them, and serve a drink to quench their inevitable thirst. (If you want to avoid eating altogether, use play dough.) A set of pretzel numerals with a matching number of small objects next to each numeral makes a nice classroom display.

Home Nibbling Challenge

Have children challenge family members to make an edible set of pretzel numerals for a special home collection. Numerals can also be made from toothpicks, sticks, play dough, clay, string, Cheerios, or almost any small food item. Any edible numerals can be eaten as a snack when the project is complete—if children don't mind seeing their work disappear!

Teeth on the Loose

Jen's lost one,
and Lan's lost two,
Now whistling loud
is fun to do.

Bo's lost three,
and Lupe four,
She keeps them hidden
in her drawer.

Tim's lost five,
and Maya six,
She shuts her mouth
when the camera clicks.

And as for me,
Well, I've lost none,
But, hey!
I feel a wiggly one!

"Teeth on the Loose"

Counting On, One More

Who Lost How Many?

Here's a perfect opportunity to personalize a poem. Rewrite the poem on chart paper. After children have recited it a number of times, replace the names in the poem with the names of volunteers from the class (and/or use names of their older siblings who may have lost more teeth). Substitutions can be made using sticky notes. Then use the poem as a springboard for discussing the concept of *one more* with questions such as the following: *Jen lost 1 tooth. Who lost 1 more tooth than Jen lost?*

Self-Portraits with Missing Teeth

Create a class collaborative book in the shape of a smile. Duplicate a copy of page 60 for each child and then cut out the smiles. Give each child a smile-shaped page on which to draw a self-portrait, coloring in gaps for missing teeth. Children should also draw their teeth that have fallen out next to their self-portraits and write the number of missing teeth. The self-portraits can be used to make a very interesting picture graph where children can visualize the concept of *one more*.

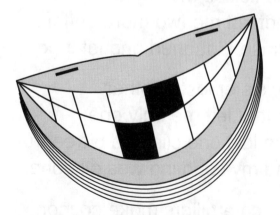

Counting on Literature

Many authors and illustrators have produced beautiful books based on counting and the concept of *one more*. Some favorites are *Rooster's Off to See the World* by Eric Carle (Picture Book Studio, 1972) and *How Many Snails?* by Paul Giganti (Greenwillow, 1988).

Counting Caterpillars

Some caterpillars crawled along,
upon the garden wall.
I watched their backs go up and down,
I counted five in all.

One critter hid behind a leaf,
Then there were only four.
I didn't really care too much
'cause there were plenty more.

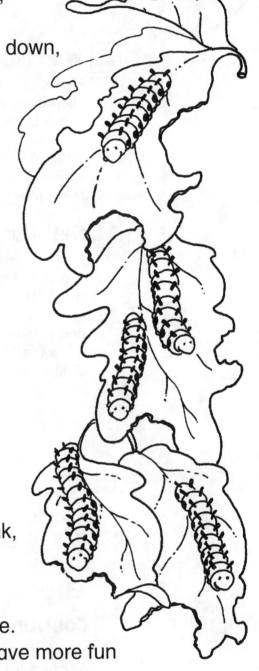

I put one in my pocket,
but it quickly crawled away.
I still had three more critters
on that sunny, summer day.

One fuzzy little fella came
and tickled my big toe.
That left me two more critters
'cause I laughed and let it go.

My sister lost another
so that left me only one.
The last one climbed a tree trunk,
and my counting was all done.

But caterpillars make cocoons
and change their shape and size.
When they have changed, I'll have more fun
by counting butterflies!

Counting Caterpillars and Other Math Poems Scholastic Professional Books

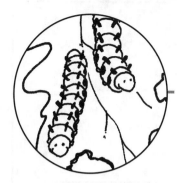

Counting Backward, One Less

Calling All Caterpillars

When reading the poem, pause before each number word and let children chime in. Then make the poem come alive by acting it out. You'll need seven actors/actresses–five caterpillars, the child playing with the caterpillars, and the child's little sister. Caterpillars can wear special hats and crawl around.

Creating Caterpillar Books

When children create their own caterpillar books, their understanding of the concept of *one less* will deepen. Of course, they can change the animal to frogs, fish, crabs, grasshoppers, lightning bugs, or other creatures that they might observe and try to catch. For each child's book, fold two sheets of 8½-inch by 11-inch paper in half and staple to form a 5½-inch by 8½-inch 4-page book. Positioning the book with the spine at the top makes it easier to illustrate. After the title page, the pages should show 5, 4, 3, 2, 1, and 0 animals—one number to a page. To make the activity more challenging, use three sheets of paper and let children start with 10 animals. Your class may enjoy reading their completed books to younger children in school or at home.

Counting All Sorts of Animals

The libraries are filled with lovely, silly, and outrageous books that illustrate the concept of *one less*. Two books with animal themes that especially work well as extensions to "Counting Caterpillars" are *Ten Sly Piranhas* by William Wise (Dial Books, 1993) and *Ten Little Crocodiles* by Colin West (Candlewick Press, 1995).

Days Till Sam's Birthday

Sam's birthday's coming very soon,
and Sam can hardly wait.
He often checks the calendar
to find the special date.
He got a button for each day
and counted one by one.
He counted very carefully
until he was all done.
He laid the buttons out again
and counted two by two.
He hoped the days till birthday time
would only be a few.
He counted them by fives and tens,
He counted many ways.
No matter how he counted them,
it came out twenty days!

Counting Caterpillars and Other Math Poems Scholastic Professional Books

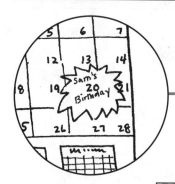

Skip Counting

▦ Naming the Number Words

There are many number words in this poem (*one* by *one*, *two* by *two*, *fives*, *tens*, *twenty*). Display the words on chart paper or a pocket chart. As you read aloud the poem, point to the number words so that children can say them with you.

You might also want to let the class personalize the poem by changing some of the words. For instance, on a chart paper version of the poem, you could use sticky notes to replace the word *birthday* with a holiday or an upcoming event. Or if a child in the class has a birthday coming up soon, substitute his or her name for Sam's name in the poem. Remember that the number *twenty* in the last line also might need to be changed.

▦ How Many Days Till . . .

Why not let 20 children in the class represent the 20 days till Sam's birthday? Have them count themselves by ones. Encourage them to group themselves in different ways and count by twos, by fives, and by tens. Next, pick an event that is 10 (or 30 days) away and count the days in different ways. The event can be as simple as an assembly, a buddy day with older buddies, an early dismissal day, a field trip, a holiday, or a full moon. As a class, for example, you could use the calendar to count the 30 days until the next field trip. Then pairs of children could connect 30 connecting cubes in groups of two and count by twos. Next, they could use the cubes to count by fives and by tens.

▦ Skip Counting Feet and Fingers

At home, have children count the number of feet in the family by ones and by twos. Then they can count the number of fingers in the family by ones, by fives, and by tens. By drawing a picture and writing out the total number of feet and fingers and how they were counted, each child will have a record to bring in, share, and compare.

Ants in Pairs

When the ants go out
to search for food,
they like to march in pairs.

It's dangerous work,
with heavy loads,
and each one does a share.

They march in twos
in long, straight lines,
They look for crumbs and scraps.

A cracker here,
a bread crumb there,
some leftovers perhaps.

And every hour,
they stop to count,
It's no time for a snooze.

Instead they grab
a partner's hand
and count themselves by twos.

When Oddly Ant
decides to come,
he likes to march in back.

They count by twos
and add on one,
And that's how they keep track.

Counting Caterpillars and Other Math Poems Scholastic Professional Books

Even and Odd Numbers

Getting Ready to March

If children have had experiences with ants—indoors and outdoors—let them tell their stories and observations. Discuss whether they've seen ants alone or in groups. As you read aloud the poem, urge children to clap (or tap or use rhythm sticks) to keep the beat. This is a lively way to emphasize the rhythm of the poem and to draw attention to the fact that the ants are marching.

Did Oddly Ant Come Along?

Have fun acting out the poem with different groups of children. Vary the number of children in each group to work with odd and even numbers. You might even make headbands with antennae for the "ants" to wear. Have the "ants" line up in pairs. If there is an odd number of ants, then one child won't have a partner. That child gets to be Oddly Ant! He or she wears a special hat or set of antennae. Whenever there is an odd number of ants, Oddly Ant marches along at the end. Whenever there is an even number of ants, Oddly stays home. For each round, ask children to count how many ants in all are marching and to determine whether the number of ants is even or odd.

Have children model the poem with black or red cubes. They can reach into a paper bag, pull out a handful of ants, and line them up in pairs. Children count the ants to see if Oddly Ant came along and tell if the number is even or odd. If you pass out copies of the poem, children can also draw and then count *more* marching ants on the copy, declaring whether the number is even or odd.

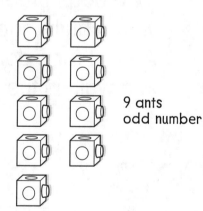

9 ants
odd number

Literature Link

Even Steven and Odd Todd/Hello Math Reader (Scholastic, 1996) is a perfect follow-up to "Ants in Pairs." This humorous book about two boys with opposite personalities takes the concept of *even* and *odd* one step farther and explores it from many different angles.

Dog Tales

Two dogs at the park bench,
Three more dogs come by,
They sniff and they yip,
but they act rather shy.

Four dogs by the oak tree,
Two dogs come along,
A few quiet growls,
but nothing goes wrong.

Three dogs on a leash,
Four dogs on their own,
They're playing and nipping
and sharing a bone.

Two dogs greet two dogs
with a high, happy bark.
A treat for a dog
is a walk in the park.

Counting Caterpillars and Other Math Poems Scholastic Professional Books

"Dog Tales"

Adding

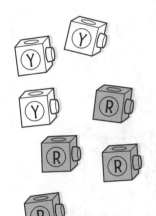

Dogs in the Pocket Chart

Ask children where they usually see dogs having fun outside and what dogs do when they get together. Prepare for the reading of the poem by having each child draw a dog on a tagboard square for the pocket chart. As you read aloud the poem, let children act it out with their dogs. Then read it again, stopping before each verse to discuss how many dogs will be needed for the upcoming verse and selecting volunteers. Have children use the dogs to create other situations such as 4 dogs meeting 1 dog. You may want to write number sentences to match the situations (e.g., 4 + 1 = 5).

Adding Pups

For this activity, children will create new addition problems and use manipulatives to represent the dogs. It will be easiest for children if each of the two groups of dog manipulatives is a different color; they can use yellow and red connecting cubes to represent two different groups of dogs, or two different kinds of beans.

Have pairs of children pull a handful of cubes from a paper bag (or toss the beans). Then children create an addition problem about dogs based on the number of manipulatives and draw a picture to record it. They can write sentences about how the dogs are interacting, along with a number sentence, for example: "3 white dogs meet 5 yellow dogs at the dog run. There are 8 dogs in all. The dogs have a fun time running up and down together! 3 + 5 = 8."

Doubling Pups

Two of Everything by Lily Toy Hong (Albert Whitman, 1993) is a Chinese folktale in which a couple discovers that anything they put in their magic pot doubles. The book provides a nice extension to the "Adding Pups" activity because doubling is an important part of addition. Encourage children to see what happens when they place their tagboard pups in a magic pot. For instance, one pair can place 3 tagboard pups into a magic pot (a hat, kitchen pot, or paper bag), while saying, "Three pups go into the pot." Another pair can show what happens next. As they say, "Six pups come out of the pot," they can make 6 pups emerge from the pot by using the 3 pups in the pot and contributing 3 more pups.

My Brother Ben's Blankey

By brother holds it
by his cheek,
and every year
it shrinks a lot.

It started out
as nine big squares,
without a rip
or dirty spot.

When Ben could walk,
the quilt was small,
Four squares was
what it had in all.

Now Ben still brings
it everywhere,
but all that's left
is one blue square.

Counting Caterpillars and Other Math Poems Scholastic Professional Books

"My Brother Ben's Blankey"

Subtracting

Counting Words

Set aside time for children to reminisce about their own *blankeys* or *loveys* or to tell about a younger sibling's treasured blanket. Write the poem on chart paper, and then with the class inspect how many words are in each line. Have children find the line with the most words (line 12). Ask, *How many more words does this line have than the line before it and the line after it?* As you recite this pert little poem with feeling, urge children to anticipate the rhyming words and chime in.

Shrinking Blankeys

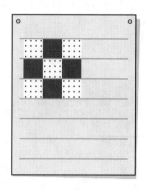

Use overhead color tiles to build Ben's blankey on an overhead projector, or re-create it on a pocket chart using nine 4-inch by 4-inch tagboard quilt squares placed in three rows of the chart.

Use the tiles or pocket chart squares to act out the poem as you read it again. You may also want to write number sentences to match the action (e.g., $9 - 5 = 4$).

Then let children use color tiles to create "blankey" subtraction problems of their own. If appropriate, have them record their subtraction problems by writing number sentences on sheets of paper. Help children group their papers by placing identical number sentences together. As a class, decide if there are any other number sentences that could be made. Don't forget $9 - 9 = 0$ and $9 - 0 = 9$.

A Bigger Blankey

Let children try making up subtraction problems using blankeys with more than nine squares. Ten squares is a magical amount because the long ten-square blankey looks like a ten frame. Ten frames are helpful visual devises for children to use since our number system is based on ten. Distribute a copy of the ten frame on page 61 to each child. Note that the blankey informally introduces the concept of area and may touch on patterns depending on how children arrange their color tiles.

Ten-Spotted Bugs

Some ten-spotted bugs
and ten-spotted frogs
and ten-spotted leopards
and turtles and dogs
all gathered together
to check out their spots
and to find all the ways
of arranging ten dots!

Sums of Ten

Ten Spots

To introduce the theme of the poem, make a tagboard ladybug with five spots on each side of a center line running down its back. Write the poem on chart paper or on pocket chart strips with the words *ten-spotted* in a different color. Draw a picture or picture card for each animal in the poem and place the picture next to its name. Display the ladybug and talk about other ways the ten spots could be arranged, such as six spots on one side and four spots on the other. Now you're ready to read the first four lines of the poem in unison! (The last four lines are less predictable). Note that there is only one punctuation mark in the whole poem and that the poem should be read accordingly.

Arranging Ten Spots

Brainstorm a list of spotted animals, including the animals named in the poem—don't forget about giraffes and geckos. Have each child draw a spotted animal—without its spots—that covers a whole sheet of paper. Ladybugs, turtles, frogs, and geckos will be easiest to draw because the picture needs to be a bird's-eye view as shown below.

Have each child draw a line down the center of the animal's back and add ten spots. They will have to decide how many dots to place on each side of the line. Ask children to record their results in number sentences, and make a list of all the number sentences. After the class studies the list, decide if *all* the ways of arranging ten spots in two groups have been found.

Ten Black Dots

Let children compile the drawings they made in the "Arranging Ten Spots" activity into a class book called *Ten-Spotted Bugs*. Discuss in which order the pictures should appear. Guide children in recognizing the pattern mentioned in the previous activity (10 + 0, 9 + 1, 8 + 2, 7 + 3, and so on). After completing this activity, children will truly appreciate Donald Crews's simple but powerful book, *Ten Black Dots* (Greenwillow, 1986).

In the Middle
(According to Terry)

My little brother tells on me,
My older sister teases.
My sister gets the privileges,
My bro' does what he pleases.
If I could choose the place I'd be,
I wouldn't choose the middle.
I'd either be the biggest one
or else I would be little.

In the Middle
(According to Chris)

My older bro' sticks up for me,
My little sister's tough.
He taught me how to bat and pitch,
She shares her toys and stuff.
If I could choose the place to be,
I'd always choose the middle.
It's hard to be the biggest
and I've already been little.

"In the Middle (According to Terry)"
"In the Middle (According to Chris)"

Graphing

Two Points of View

On an overhead projector, chart paper, or an extrawide pocket chart, display a written version of the poem. This may help children spot the pattern–both poems have the same title, the same number of lines, and a similar line structure. What's different about each poem is the attitude of each narrator. Query children about the position they occupy in their families—first, middle, or last—and the pluses and minuses of each position.

Oldest, Middle, Youngest

Start with a people graph. Tape the headings *first, middle,* and *last* to the floor and then have children line up behind each heading depending on their positions in their families. Next create a more permanent picture graph by having each child draw a picture of himself or herself to place under the same headings. Discuss which category has the greatest number of children and which has the least number, and how you can tell by looking. Direct children to find out how many are in each category. Ask how they would figure out how many more children are in one category than in another.

First, Second, Third, . . .

At home, have children draw pictures of their siblings and themselves, labeling each by ordinal numbers according to position—*first, second, third,* and so on. Urge children to ask their parents to do the same activity. They can then study their parents' drawings and figure out if a parent was the first, second, third, . . . child in the family.

Bushy-Tailed Mathematicians

The squirrels kept their walnuts
in a giant saving jar,
When the jar was full, they counted
all the walnuts saved so far.

First they grouped them all by tens
and then they counted one and all,
Though it took them several hours,
all the squirrels had a ball.

When the walnuts were all counted,
then the squirrels used a pen,
wrote the total on a leaf and
put them in the jar again.

They decided not to eat them
though they had a large amount,
'cause their favorite thing with walnuts
is to group by tens and count.

Counting Caterpillars and Other Math Poems Scholastic Professional Books

"Bushy-Tailed Mathematicians"

Place Value

Saving Walnuts, Saving Pennies

Though the poem is not an easy read, children can have fun interacting with it. Let them anticipate the rhyming words at the ends of the verses and encourage them to chant with enthusiasm. Write the poem on chart paper and then do some word substitutions. Change the word *squirrels* to *children*, *walnuts* to *pennies*, and *eat* to *spend*. The class will have a whole new poem (and math skill) to think about!

Count to Ten and Begin Again

Ten frames, which were created to help children visualize number and place value, are perfect for this poem. Make a copy of page 62 for each child and distribute.

Set up several counting stations. For each station provide a jar filled with pennies, little pinecones, stones, or whatever is abundant in your area that will fit on ten frames. To count stones, for example, groups of children can fill up as many ten frames as possible and find how many in all.

10 Ten Frames

With older children, you can go farther by using pennies in the jar and letting them trade for a dime every time they fill up a ten frame. When all the pennies have been counted and traded, they can find the total amount of money in the jar.

Pennies in Pockets and Purses

Ask children to find out how many pennies their parents have at home in pockets and purses and record the number. The next day at school, have them use single strips from graph paper to draw all the pennies they found at home. Tape all the strips together. Let children take turns cutting the strips after each group of ten. Count by tens to find the total number of pennies.

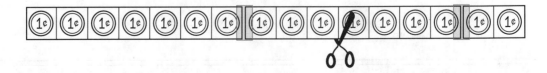

One Hundred All Year Long

On a weekend day in springtime,
one hundred boats are on the bay.
Grab your hat and you can join them
for a wet and wavy day.

In the summer when you're camping,
one hundred lights can fill the sky.
There is nothing quite as special
as a blinking firefly.

When you're walking to the schoolyard
in the brilliant autumn sun,
you may crunch one hundred leaflets—
it can be a lot of fun.

On a snowy slope in winter,
you may see one hundred sleds.
You can warm yourself with cocoa
when you finally go to bed.

Counting Caterpillars and Other Math Poems   Scholastic Professional Books

One Hundred

One Hundred in Each Season

Add this poem to your collection of literature to celebrate the hundredth day of school. Explain that the poem describes one hundred things that a child might see during each season of the year. Brainstorm a list of things that children might see one hundred of—stars, baseball cards, stickers in a sticker book, tadpoles in a pond, leaves on a tree, pennies in a jar, and so on—and talk about in which season they might see each group of objects. As you read aloud the poem, remind children to listen for the seasonal clues.

On an overhead transparency or chart paper version of the poem, allow children to interact with the poem. Leave out the words *boats* and *sleds* in the first and last verses. Let children think of replacement words, such as *surfers* and *snowflakes*. The other verses can be changed as well, but it's a little more involved. If children want to make up completely new verses, the verses need not rhyme.

One Hundred Fingers

Create a mural of children's handprints containing one hundred poster-paint fingers. Let the class figure out how many children can participate in printing their hands on the mural. (Creating two murals will ensure that each child gets to participate at least once.) Ask children to count by fives and by tens to make sure the mural really shows one hundred fingers.

Collecting One Hundred

For homework, have children make a collection of one hundred of the same items to bring in the next day in a self-seal bag. Make sure parents know that anything will do–leaves, beans, Styrofoam pieces, Cheerios, pennies, and so on. Using paper cups in the classroom, children can recount each other's items by grouping them by fives and tens. Then read the book *One Hundred Hungry Ants* by Elinor J. Pinczes (Houghton Mifflin, 1994) to children. They'll especially appreciate the story after they have collected and counted one hundred items.

Estimating Chicken Pox

I estimate my chicken pocks,
at a million pocks or more.
But when I really count them all,
they total thirty-four.

My brother caught my chicken pox
and he was itching, too.
But my very lucky brother got
two pocks and he was through.

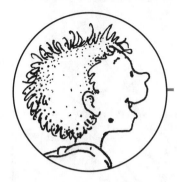

Estimating/ Large Numbers

 ## Zillions of Chicken Pox

Solicit children's experiences with chicken pox, mosquito or chigger bites, or poison oak or ivy. Make sure the class understands that some children get lots of chicken pocks or bites and others get only a few. Ask: *Did it ever feel like you had a million pocks, bites, or itches? About how many were there when you really counted?*

After you read aloud the poem, let children make suggestions for numbers that may be substituted for *a million* in line two, such as *a thousand, a hundred thousand, a billion,* or *a trillion.* Share the fact with children that a *zillion* is not really a number, but a *googol* is. It means the numeral 1 followed by one hundred zeros.

 ## Estimating Festival

Put on an estimation festival in your classroom! Let pairs of children create estimating challenges to exchange with classmates. Make sure pairs have sheets of paper to record their estimates for the challenges. You may want to get the ball rolling with a traditional estimating jar such as a large glass jar filled with marbles or beans. To help children think of interesting challenges, suggest the following challenges:

- Estimate how many hands will fit on this piece of paper.
- Estimate how long the window is if you use connecting cubes to measure it.

In keeping with the spirit of the poem, children may even draw a child with lots of chicken pox or mosquito bites and ask about how many pocks or bites there are.

 ## Estimating Backpacks

Create an "Estimating Backpack" that children can alternate taking home. Place a copy of the poem and a jar or plastic bag filled with small items in the backpack. Include a brief instruction sheet asking the child and family members to estimate the number of items in the jar and then count to see who made the closest estimate.

Gardening with Snails

Two rows of daisies,
with three in each row.
I dug and I watered
and left them to grow.

I planted some pumpkins
in four rows of two.
I built a big scarecrow
and then I was through.

At night, twenty snails
marched out on the lawn,
and early next morning
my plants were all gone.

I'll have to find plants
that the snails don't attack,
'cause they think that my garden's
a great midnight snack!

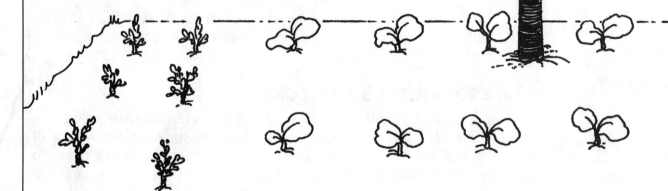

Counting Caterpillars and Other Math Poems Scholastic Professional Books

Pre-Multiplication

Planting the Garden

Re-create the first two verses of "Gardening with Snails" on a pocket chart or chart paper and prepare to play with the poem. Make a small picture card for each daisy and pumpkin plant. Using the poem as a guide, children can show 2 rows with 3 daisies in each row and 4 rows with 2 pumpkins in each row. Give them a chance to determine how many daisies and how many pumpkins are in the garden. Of course, children might want to plant different flowers or vegetables. If so, let them substitute new plant names in the poem and draw the appropriate picture cards. They also might want to change the number of rows and the number of plants in each row; for example, they might have 3 rows of corn with 5 plants in each row.

How Does Your Garden Grow?

Give children a chance to plant their own gardens in rows. They can draw their gardens or use torn colored paper to represent the plants. You may also want to supply cut vegetables and tempera paint so children may make veggie prints. Direct them to write how many rows, how many plants in each row, and how many plants in all under their pictures. To add pizzazz to the activity, let children plant fast-growing nasturtiums in paper cups. Place the cups on trays, in different arrangements. Have children figure out how many plants are on each tray.

Literature Link

Join author Joy N. Hulme for a beautiful visit to the sea as she explores pre-multiplication in *Sea Squares* (Hyperion, 1991). The clever, rhyming verse and the luscious illustrations are sure to deepen children's understanding of multiplication as repeated addition.

Dividing up Bugs

Teresa keeps a lot of bugs
in jars upon her floor.
There's barely any place to step,
It's hard to shut her door.

The last time that she counted bugs,
they totaled twenty-four.
But every week that passes by,
she adds a couple more.

Each time she finds a nifty bug,
she finds a matching one.
She says with two in every jar,
they seem to have more fun.

Two beetles here, two squash bugs there,
some moths and crickets, too.
Two dragonflies, two ladybugs,
two flies that look bright blue.

She frees them after several days,
It's only right to do.
When she grows up, she says she'll run
a giant insect zoo!

Counting Caterpillars and Other Math Poems Scholastic Professional Books

Pre-Division

Rhymes with Zoo

This poem contains many cool rhyming words. Have children brainstorm lists of words that rhyme with *floor*, *one*, and *zoo*. Then they can listen for the rhyming words as you read aloud the poem. But don't start quite yet. First make two large flashcards, one with the word *bug* and one with the word *bugs*, to display. Ask children to join in whenever the word *bug* or *bugs* comes up in the poem.

Dividing up Insects

The poem is really a poetic word problem with the question, "How many jars of bugs did Teresa have in her room at last count?" Read the poem again, and have children listen for the information they need to solve the problem (24 bugs, 2 in each jar). Provide beans for bugs and paper cups for jars. Pairs of children can put the 24 bugs in the jars and find how many jars are needed to house them all. Note that it may be helpful to the bug world to tell children to free bugs after one day, as Teresa does, if they decide to have insect zoos of their own.

More Bugs in Each Jar

To extend the activity, set up a learning center with some "What if. . ." questions:

- *What if Teresa collects 24 bugs and puts 3 bugs in each jar?*
- *What if Teresa collects 16 bugs and puts 4 in each jar?*
- *What if she collects 26 bugs and puts 5 in each jar?*
  (Hmm—one critter would have to be alone.)

No Ruler? No Problem!

I measured using hand spans,
and my notebook came out two.
When a ruler isn't handy,
then a hand or foot will do.

My cat was twenty thumb prints,
and my dog was twenty-eight.
When I cannot find my ruler,
then my thumb print works just great.

I measured using arm spans,
and my bedroom came out four.
There are lots of ways to measure—
arms and hands and many more!

Counting Caterpillars and Other Math Poems Scholastic Professional Books

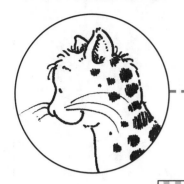

Measuring

What's a Handy Ruler?

Share the title of the poem with children and let them try to imagine what it's about. Once they've figured it out, brainstorm a list of rulers they "carry with them" at all times–hand spans, arm spans, strides, baby steps, thumb lengths, body lengths, and cubits (from the elbow to the tip of fingers).

Baby Steps Across the Rug

Pair children and challenge them to measure objects and distances in the classroom (or the schoolyard) using their body rulers. How many baby steps across is the rug? How many strides does it take to cross the classroom? How many hand spans or thumb lengths is the desk? Why are there more thumb lengths than hand spans?

You can also turn around the questions! Ask children if they can find something in the classroom that is 2 arm spans long, 5 thumb lengths long, 6 cubits long, or 10 hand spans long.

For extra fun, line up all the children outside the classroom door. Have them stretch their arms and touch each other's fingertips. What is the length, in arm spans, of the class? To find the length to the nearest foot, draw a chalk line from the first child to the last child and then measure it.

Inching Along

Leo Lionni's charming book *Inch by Inch* (Astor-Honor, 1995) presents some interesting problems for an inchworm asked to measure the beak, neck, tail, and legs of various winged predators. Eventually, he's challenged to measure the song of a nightingale! Children can make a large drawing of a bird based on the story and measure parts of it using *Inchworms* or nonstandard units such as Unifix Cubes or connecting cubes. A nice discussion can ensue about how they might go about measuring a song. (They could time it; write the musical notes on paper and measure them; count how many beats or how many notes.)

Birthday Money

Ted's auntie gave him birthday cash,
He's not sure what to do.
He might see movies all day long
and bring a friend or two.

He just might buy some comic books
or candy at the store.
He might treat friends to ice cream cones—
he'll have to think some more.

Oh no, don't say it, please be wrong,
Please say it isn't true.
He has to pay for the window
that his soccer ball went through!

Counting Caterpillars and Other Math Poems   Scholastic Professional Books

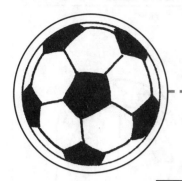

Money

▦ Rhythmic Reading

Ask children if they'd rather receive money or a gift as a birthday present, and why. When you're ready to read the poem, explain that "Birthday Money" has a nice rhythm to it. Have children clap or use rhythm sticks to keep time to the beat. For fun, they can click the sticks together for the first six beats and click them on the floor for the seventh beat.

▦ Catalog Shopping

Let children create catalogs and order items. Either you or the children can draw pictures for the catalog page, or the pictures can be cut from magazines. Items should be priced from 2¢ to 20¢, depending on the grade level. Give children play money coins, or real coins, and ask them to decide which item(s) they want to buy. The amount of money they have to spend will depend on the grade level (e.g., 10¢ in pennies for kindergarten, 25¢ for grade 1, 50¢ or more for grade 2). Children can record their purchases using words or pictures. They should also record the prices of the items they buy. Consider having a banker who exchanges nickels and dimes for pennies.

▦ Shopping Spree

It's daydreaming time! Read *Alexander Who Used to Be Rich Last Sunday* by Judith Viorst (Atheneum, 1978). Discuss with children how they would spend a gift of money. Set the amount at $5, $50, or $100. Have them write about and illustrate what they would do with their money. Encourage children to use their imaginations but to be as specific as possible. Set aside time so everyone has a chance to share his or her shopping spree daydreams.

A Perfect Saturday

I woke at eight
and watched a show,
Then half past nine,
I played with Joe.
At twelve o'clock
we ate some food,
and got into
a baseball mood.
At five, we picked
a house to sleep,
We promised not to
make a peep.
At nine, we heard,
"Goodnight, you guys."
At ten, we finally
closed our eyes.
The whole day long
on Saturday,
the only thing
we did was play.
So you can see
why Saturday
was such an all-round
perfect day!

Counting Caterpillars and Other Math Poems Scholastic Professional Books

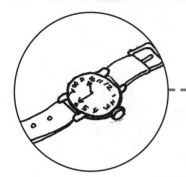

Time

Lively Rhythm to the Day

Open up discussion of a topic children can relate to enthusiastically—favorite days of the week. Encourage them to elaborate on the reasons for their choices and then make a graph to show the results. Notice that the poem has a nice pattern to it, especially the first sixteen lines. For the second read-through, ask children to repeat each line after you.

Plan a Perfect Day

Talk about the different times in the poem and have children show them on clocks with movable hands. (For older children, you might want to change some of the times to a quarter after, half past, or a quarter to the hour.) Let children plan a perfect day, in pictures and/or in writing, from the time they get up to the time they go to bed. Emphasize that their plans should include the time of day, either in numbers or on a clockface. Duplicate and cut out page 63 for children. They can draw the hands on the clockfaces and draw or write about an activity in the space to the right of each clock.

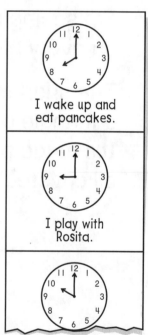

I wake up and eat pancakes.

I play with Rosita.

Rise and Shine on Saturday

Have children figure out what time they usually wake up on Saturdays. If necessary, give them time to consult with family members at home. Then make a graph of the times, using the graph paper on page 59. Discuss the graph with the class. Ask questions such as the following: *What is the most popular time? What is the earliest time? What is the latest time?*

Shadow Shapes

I'm stepping on a triangle,
I hop onto a square.
The shadow shapes on sunny days
are lying everywhere.

My hat looks like a triangle.
My arm looks like one, too.
I'm seeing lots of rectangles
on every block or two.

The shadow of that cat is not
a triangle or square.
It's made of lots of different shapes
all covered up with hair!

2-Dimensional Shapes

Searching for Shape Words

Write a list of 2-dimensional shape names on chart paper or the board. After you pass out a copy of the poem to each child, read the title of the poem together and notice that both words start with the phoneme *sh*. Give children a chance to use the title as a clue for guessing what the poem is about. Then ask them to hunt for and underline the shape words in the poem.

Searching for Shadow Shapes

At this age level could include circles, squares, rectangles, triangles, and diamonds. Parallelograms and other four-sided shapes can also be explored, if appropriate.

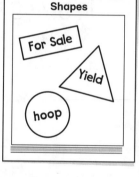

Go outdoors and let children draw and/or record the names of objects that are 2-dimensional shapes. Make copies of the Shapes sheet on page 64 for children to use. Of course, the shadows of the objects can be inspected as well. Look for "For Sale" signs (rectangles), yield signs (triangles), and basketball hoops (circle). For contrast, ask children which objects and shadows are not geometric. Natural objects such as trees, bushes, and animals fit in this category.

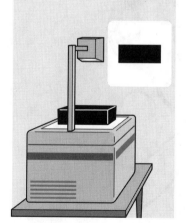

Indoors, you can show children pattern blocks, geoblocks, boxes, cans, and other geometric objects and have them predict what shapes the shadows will make on the overhead projector. Demonstrate how to create the sides of triangles, squares, rectangles, and diamonds on the overhead projector with your fingers. Allow time for children to try their hand at making shadow shapes.

Then, as a follow-up to the last verse of the poem, have children construct a cat from pattern blocks.

Literature Link

In *The Shape of Things* by Dayle Ann Dodds (Candlewick Press, 1994), the author describes a number of objects in the world that are made of combinations of shapes. The book serves as a delightful invitation for children to build recognizable objects from pattern blocks.

Bubble Trouble

When I'm blowing a bubble,
it's always a sphere—

With a dipper that's square,
rounded bubbles appear.

With a three-sided dipper,
I still get round bubbles.

Blowing bubbly cubes
is giving me troubles!

3-Dimensional Shapes

Blowing Bubbly Bubbles

Before you begin reading the poem, gather props to accompany it. Collect a gallery of solid shapes–a sphere, a cube, a rectangular solid, a cone, a cylinder, and a pyramid. (For younger children, the names *ball*, *box, cone, can*, and *pyramid* work well.) Make a bubble mixture of liquid detergent and water and set it out with circular, square, and triangular dippers. The dippers can be made from tagboard covered with tape or from transparency paper as shown.

Before reading aloud the poem to children, be aware that it is a bit of a tongue twister. Show the poem on the overhead projector, chart paper, or a pocket chart. After reading it once, repeat each line again and let children say the line after you. Ask them to find all the places in the poem where a form of the word *bubble* appears.

Fantastic Bubbles

Display the solid shape collection again. Then study and discuss each dipper. Ask which solid shape of bubble might come out of each shape dipper. To answer these questions, children will have to carefully observe the shapes of the faces of the solids. For instance, they may guess that bubbles in the shapes of cubes or rectangular solids might come out of the square dipper. Then have them blow single bubbles with all the dippers. All the bubbles will be spheres! This is because a bubble wants to take up the least space possible and use the least energy possible. The shape that meets these requirements is a sphere.

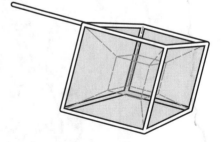

You *can*, however, make a square bubble in the middle of other bubbles! Create the skeleton of a cube using pipe cleaners or Wikki Stix as shown.

The Solid Shape Factory

Stock various locations around the classroom with materials where children can make 3-dimensional shapes. Give them time to visit the stations. At a toothpick and marshmallow station, children can make shapes such as cubes and pyramids. At a paper and tape station, children can roll and tape paper to make cylinders and cones. A cone can be folded from a circle that has been cut along one radius.

Surprising Symmetry

On leaves,
On bugs,
On butterflies,
Both sides are
quite the same.
But if you ask
your mother why,
she really can't explain.

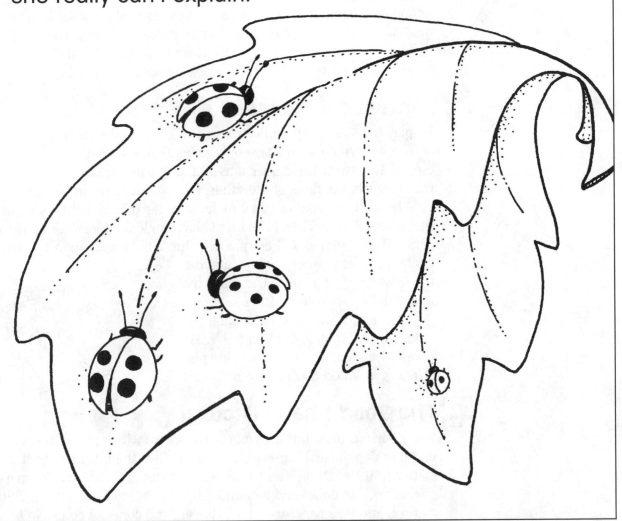

Counting Caterpillars and Other Math Poems Scholastic Professional Books

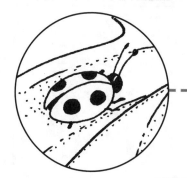

Symmetry

▦ Picturing the Poem

Create three large symmetrical pictures of a leaf, a butterfly, and a lady-bug on tagboard. As you and your class recite the poem together, let three children at a time hold up the appropriate pictures. As you repeat the poem, substitute a different person for *mother* with each reading. Try *father*, *teacher*, *brother*, *sister*, *grandma*, and *grandpa*.

▦ Symmetry Surprise

Encourage children to experience symmetry in the making. Have them paint half of a butterfly, ladybug, or leaf on one side of a sheet of paper that has a fold down the middle. While the paint is still wet, have children fold, press, and then open the paper. They will find a beautiful symmetrical painting. In the same vein, each child can use pattern blocks to create a design on one half of a sheet of paper that has a fold line. The child, or the child's partner, can complete the pattern block design by creating a mirror image on the other side of the line.

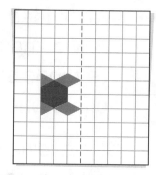

▦ Natural Symmetry

For a homework exploration, encourage children and family members to collect leaves from the neighborhood. Have them show their family that both sides of the leaf are the same or nearly the same. Ask children to bring in their two favorite leaves so they can study them and find the veins (lines of symmetry) that run down the middle and split the leaves in half. (Using a magnifying glass to find the vein can be exciting!) The leaves can be ironed between two pieces of waxed paper and hung in the classroom as examples of symmetry in nature. With a rectangular mirror, children can also create symmetrical surprises by placing the mirror next to or on top of a leaf or other objects.

Sharing a Room

Sally Sue is very messy,
She leaves toys thrown everywhere.
She's got laundry on her bookshelf,
gobs of toothpaste on her chair.

As for me, I'm neat and tidy,
I have labels on each drawer.
Every day I use the vacuum,
You could eat right off my floor.

We divided up the bedroom,
drew a line across the floor.
We made sure that it was even,
neither one was getting more.

She allows me in the closet,
and I let her use the door.
Though the plan is not quite perfect,
it's much better than before!

Counting Caterpillars and Other Math Poems Scholastic Professional Books

Fractions

Sharing a Room

Any child who shares a bedroom will have plenty to say about this poem. List children's grievances along with the benefits of sharing a room. Write the first verse on chart paper or a pocket chart so that children can make it their own. Challenge them to substitute new words for *toys*, *laundry*, and *gobs of toothpaste*. Use a sticky note for each substitution.

Dividing the Room

A geoboard and rubber bands can inspire creativity in children. They can work with the geoboards to find ways to divide a bedroom (the geoboard) in half. Instruct children to record their designs on dot paper. Share ideas and find out how many different ways the class discovered to divide the "geoboard room" in half.

Furnishing the Divided Room

Give children rectangular pieces of paper and let them find ways to divide the room in half again—this time, by folding the paper. They may divide the room using a vertical or horizontal fold.

Some children may fold along the diagonal. Still others may branch out and find an unusual strategy such as dividing the paper into 4 equal rectangles and giving two rectangles each to Child 1 and Child 2.

Child 1	Child 2
Child 2	Child 1

Finally, ask children to draw furniture in the room, showing where a bed, desk, and bookshelf for each roommate would go. Some children will be ready for an extension activity such as dividing their "paper rooms" equally among three or four siblings.

APPENDIX

Bird Patterns
Graph Paper
Smile Template
Ten Frame
10 Ten Frames
Clockfaces
Shapes

Bird Patterns

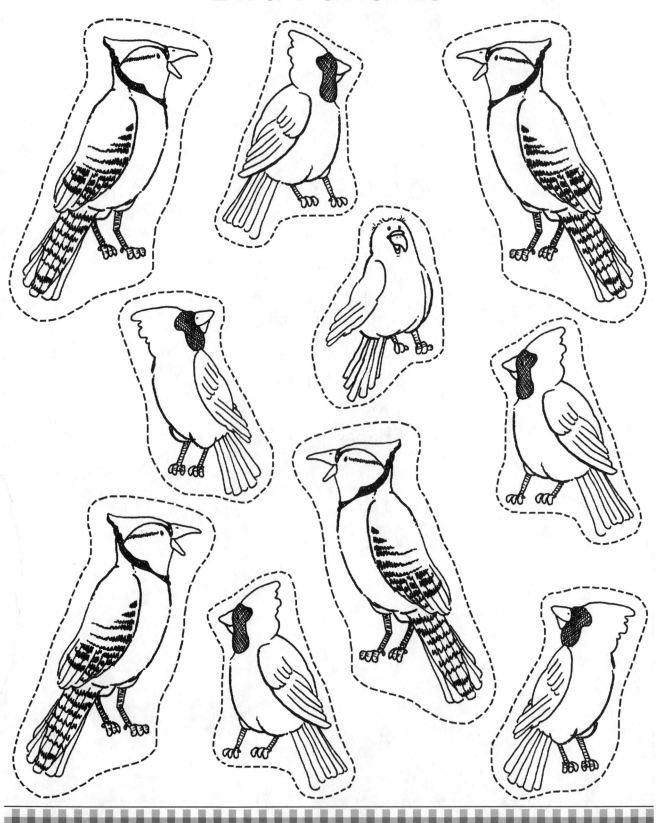

Graph Paper

Smile Template

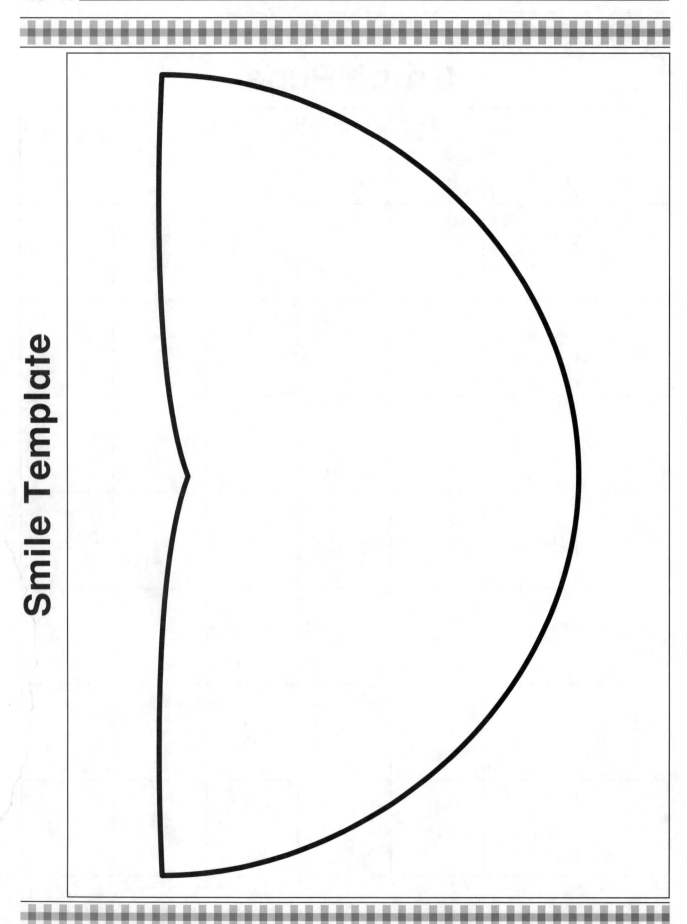

Ten Frame

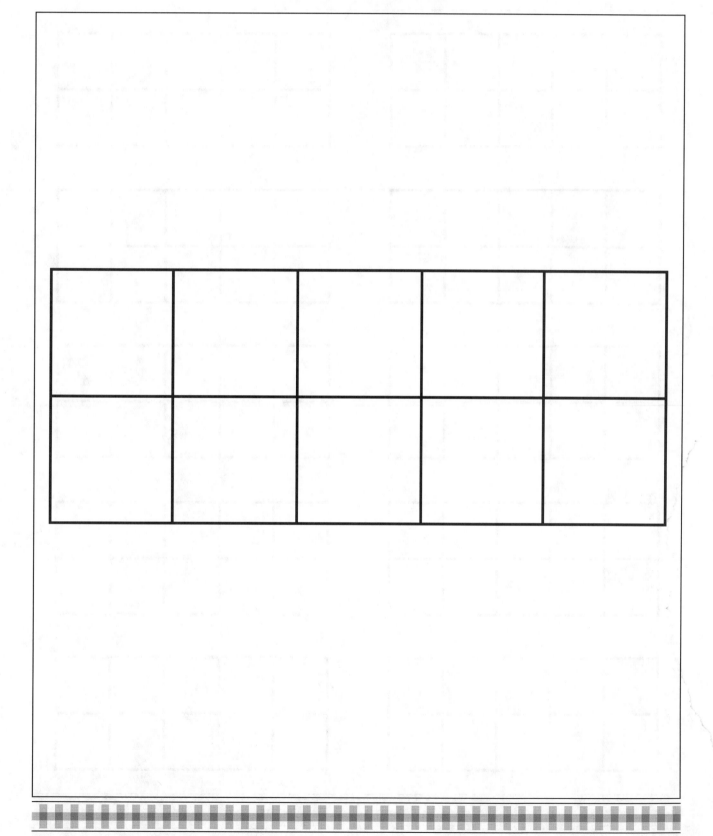

10 Ten Frames

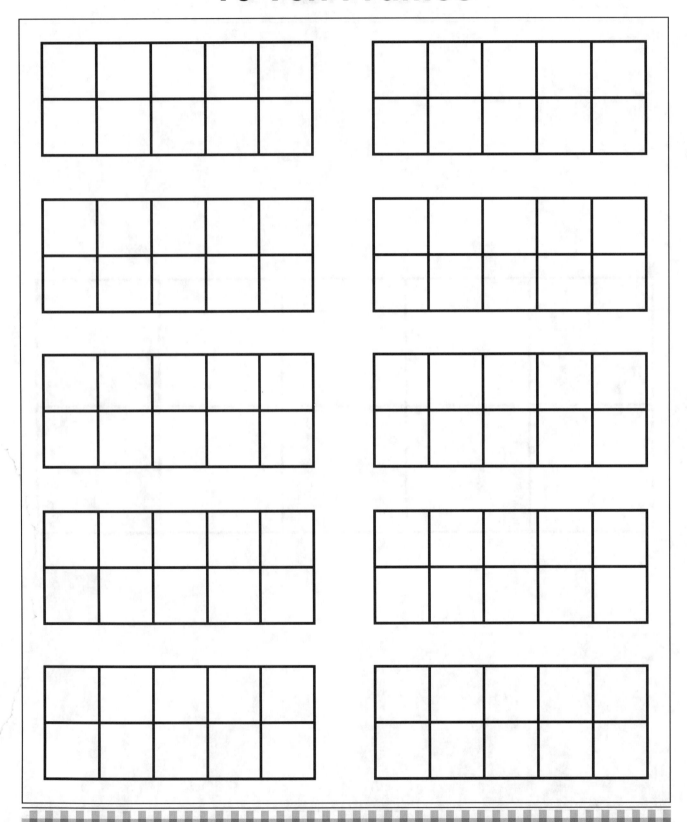

Counting Caterpillars and Other Math Poems Scholastic Professional Books

Clockfaces

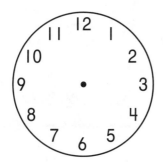

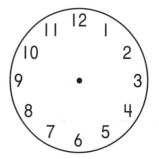

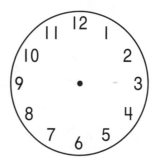

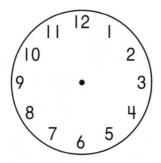

Shapes